Tarot

Enter the fascinating world of the ancient Tarot

Sasha Fenton

H·M

This revised edition published in the UK in 2002 by
Haldane Mason Ltd
PO Box 34196, London NW10 3YB
email: haldane.mason@dial.pipex.com

ISBN: 1-902463-78-1

A HALDANE MASON BOOK
Art Director: Ron Samuel
Editor: Christopher Fagg
Design: Rachel Clark, Zoë Mellors
Illustrator: Samantha Bale

Printed in China

*Material from this book previously
published in* Tarot*, ISBN: 1-84067-083-5*

CONTENTS

THE TAROT CARDS

The actual origin of the Tarot is obscure and, although many people think that the cards originated in Egypt, there is some reason to suspect that they came from China. Paper was manufactured in both ancient Egypt and later in ancient China (using different processes), but each civilization had its own tradition of using illustrations to depict ideas and events.

Whatever the original source, the cards travelled westwards into southern Europe during the 14th century with travelling peoples, some of whom came via Egypt, which may be why such people became known as 'gypsies'. Thus the images that have been handed down to modern Tarot card readers are those of life in the courts and the rural communities of those medieval European cultures.

The influence of the original Tarot images spread far and wide, so that even today the figurative designs of chess pieces and playing cards derive from the traditional Tarot deck.

Tarot reading has been in and out of favour many times but now it is a popular pastime and there is no longer anything "occult" or sinister about it. I have carefully written this book in such a way that anyone can safely use it.

Each card embodies a story and many of them refer back to symbolic medieval figures or ideas but, when reading the cards today, we have to consider the relevance that they have to life as we know it now. In fact, part of the challenge of the Tarot is to make people think creatively about their lives and situations. By imaginatively interpreting the old stories embodied in the cards to reflect current realities, you can find new ways of looking at the events and personalities which surround you in your daily life.

The 78-card Tarot pack is divided into two categories, known as the Major and Minor Arcana. The character of a Tarot reading is influenced by the combinations in which these two categories appear as the cards are dealt. The 22 Major Arcana cards each embody powerful symbols and, when a proportionately greater number of these turn up in a reading, fateful changes loom in the future. The 56 Minor Arcana cards relate more to daily life, and, if a reading is dominated by them, the questioner is unlikely to be facing radical changes. However, even one or two Major Arcana cards standing out in a spread must be taken seriously.

The Minor Arcana is divided into four suits called Wands, Cups, Pentacles and Swords, and each of these suits has a character of its own. The court cards—the King, Queen, Knight and Page—represent characters which may affect one's life, but they can also illustrate an atmosphere or an environment. For example, a number of Cup court cards in a spread suggests an aura of love, companionship and support.

You can choose to keep your cards in the upright position (where all the cards appear the right way up to you) at all times, giving the positive aspects of each card. Or you may prefer to use both the upright and the reversed positions (where the cards appear upside-down to you), which combine positive and negative aspects. I have outlined the positive and negative aspects of every card in the pack. The stories you make can be simple or complex. The choice of reading style is yours.

THE MAJOR ARCANA

The name *Arcana* is connected to the words *arcane* and *ancient* but these words themselves hark back to distant pagan origins. As we have seen, the Major Arcana itself is made up of 22 cards, sometimes referred to as trump cards. Each of these major Arcana cards has a particularly deep and important meaning, and they portray powerful, dynamic images of change, justice, difficulty, strength, joy and so forth. These basic ideas are then amplified in greater detail by the more specific messages contained within the Minor Arcana cards that usually surround them in any reading.

The Fool

The Magician

The High Priestess

The Empress

The Emperor

The Hierophant

The Lovers

The Chariot

Strength

The Hermit

The oldest surviving examples of the Major Arcana carry stark medieval images still used in many packs. These days there are many different variations of the Tarot, on themes ranging from King Arthur to Shakespeare. In this book, the imagery is taken from medieval illuminated manuscripts. Whatever the imagery, the richness of their stories and associations make the Tarot cards endlessly fascinating.

Tarot cards are still used for game-playing in parts of Spain and Italy. In these *Taroc* or *Tarocco* decks, all but one of the Major Arcana cards (the Fool) have been dropped from the deck. Ordinary playing cards are another spin-off, invented in France in the 17th century. Each suit contains three court cards, with the Jack in place of the Knight and the Page dropped altogether, while the Fool is retained as the Joker.

The Fool

Number: 0

Key ideas: *A fresh start. A new concept.*

The Fool

POSITIVE

The figure on this card is of an innocent youngster setting out on a journey; indeed in many Tarot decks he appears to be stepping over the edge of a cliff! The character is optimistic, innocent and ingenuous, and he has a lot to learn. The Fool card refers to the start of a new love relationship, a business venture, a course of education, a significant journey, or indeed any kind of beginning. The feeling is optimistic, as it suggests that the forthcoming enterprise will bring more than its fair share of joy and success.

There is an element of fun surrounding this card, and it suggests that innocence and a willingness to try new things will be more useful than a world-weary and cynical attitude. Protection and spiritual guidance will be around you. The number zero on this card reminds us that in life and even in death, there is no real beginning or end, so the Fool represents the start of a new phase of your soul's journey.

NEGATIVE

Think before acting because a proposed new project may encounter a few drawbacks, although things should work out well enough in the end. Alternatively, your idea may be fine, but it will be a while before the project gets off the ground. Avoid bad company and keep to the straight and narrow because stupid or self-destructive behaviour will bring a downfall. Examine your motives before making a start on anything new—even learning the Tarot!

The Magician

Number: 1

Key ideas: *Market your skills.*
Real or apparent confidence.

The Magician

POSITIVE

This card depicts a Magician who has all the elements of the Tarot pack to hand, these being the Cup, Wand, Sword and Pentacle, and he understands how to use them. On a purely practical level, this suggests that you are about to embark on a new enterprise and it is one that you are well equipped to carry out. You actually have the knowledge, skills and experience at hand but you must now concentrate on using these skills and also on marketing them. There is a suggestion that, even if you don't feel confident, you should do your best to appear so, and you may need to use a touch of trickery to get what you want. Time upon time, I see this card appear when a client is about to become self-employed.

In a spiritual context, this card shows that it is time to put intuition and psychic abilities to good use. The Magician can also announce the imminent arrival of an important man into the life of a woman, and in this case, the man will be amusing and intelligent.

NEGATIVE

The message here is to avoid trickery, both by being strictly ethical in your own behaviour and by guarding against manipulation and lies from other quarters. The card also exhorts you not to overlook or to back away from an opportunity for advancement. If the Magician represents a new lover, watch out—he may be tricky!

The High Priestess

Number: 2

Key ideas: *Cool logic and intuition. Teaching or learning.*

The High Priestess

POSITIVE

The Priestess often turns up when a period of study is in the pipeline and it suggests that you are about to spend some time learning a new concept or getting to grips with a new skill. Alternatively, it suggests that you yourself will shortly be passing on the benefit of your knowledge to others. The figure on the cards is a cool and knowledgeable woman who is a well of spiritual understanding. This card can suggest the start of a period of training in the Tarot, clairvoyance, astrology or something similar. I often find the Priestess appearing when clients are intuitive or psychic themselves.

The Priestess tells you that something has yet to be revealed and that you are not in possession of the full facts. She advises you to tackle future problems by means of logic and intuition, rather than to allow emotions such as anger or jealousy to take over. Another interpretation is that a good female friend or mentor is about to enter your life.

NEGATIVE

Raw emotion will cloud your thinking. Another suggestion is that you are so self-absorbed that you can't or won't see the needs of those who are around you. There may be a suggestion that you need to improve your sexual technique!

The Empress

Number: 3

Key ideas: *Abundance and fruitfulness.*
A feminine, motherly person.

The Empress

POSITIVE

The picture on this card often depicts a very feminine woman surrounded by ripening corn, fruit and flowers, suggesting that a period of abundance is on the way. Just as the previous card suggested spiritual or mental development, this one brings success in practical and worldly matters. Hopes will come to fruition and you will begin to feel more confident while reaping the rewards of your efforts. Finances will soon improve.

A male questioner will shortly meet a loving woman while a female questioner will soon have a kind female friend. This is a warmly emotional card, suggesting love and comfort. If a marriage is planned, there will be much happiness, and the joyful situation could include the birth of a child. If you don't want children yourself, there might be a new baby around you soon.

Finally, if you are considering a move of house, your new home will be in a pleasant area with a well-kept garden and a nice outlook and there may be farmland or woods nearby.

NEGATIVE

Practical and financial problems connected to property, land, a garden or premises of any kind are likely. There may be a temporary shortage of money due to laziness or over-spending. In some cases, a battle with an avaricious woman could be the cause of financial hardship and this scenario is typical of a difficult divorce. The Empress can signify problems related to fertility or the loss of a baby through miscarriage or abortion. Sometimes this card simply suggests that the happiness that you are waiting for will come, but not just yet.

The Emperor

Number: 4

Key ideas: *Will-power. Decision making. An executive person.*

The Emperor

POSITIVE

The figure on this card is of a powerful man who is in a strong position. This card stands for material status and earthly wisdom, rather than spiritual knowledge. The suggestion is that you will soon be in a much stronger position at work, with a possible promotion to a position of authority. If you are seeking employment this is an optimistic card to draw because it shows that something worthwhile is on the way, bringing more money and an increase of status. If you aren't interested in a career, your status is still set to rise and you will feel far more in control, even if this is only within your own household.

Often the Emperor refers to an influential or authoritative person such as a husband or father figure. The man has a good position in life and he is confident about his abilities, but there is a slight warning not to become involved with a bossy or controlling person!

NEGATIVE

If you want to improve your status or financial situation, you must put your shoulder to the wheel because nothing will come along without hard work. Improvements will come, but not just yet. Weakness, sickness or laziness may hold you back. If there is a new face coming on to the scene, then this man is not all that he claims to be!

The Hierophant

Number: 5

Key ideas: *A teacher or mentor. Traditional values.*

The Hierophant

POSITIVE

The figure depicted here is a religious one, suggesting that the power and knowledge held in this card are spiritual rather than practical or material. There are a number of possible meanings to this card, depending upon your circumstances. The first is that if you need a teacher, counsellor or guide, this person will soon come along. If you are keen to get in contact with a spiritual guide, you should soon do so. Whether from the earthly plane or 'the other side', good advice is on the way.

Another interpretation is that the Hierophant advises you to act in a particularly ethical manner, even to be a little old-fashioned and straight-laced in your future dealings. Casual arrangements in business or in personal life will become firm commitments and a wedding may be on the way. If you are hanging about and waiting for something to happen, it soon will.

NEGATIVE

In all future dealings, you must guard against sloppiness and you must do the right thing for the right reasons. You must also guard against being too kind or too generous, especially if you are doing so for the sake of peace. Putting your foot down might be a better option. Finally, if you have become stuck in a rut of routine or tradition, you will shortly find a way of surprising your loved ones.

The Lovers

Number: 6

Key ideas: *Love. Beauty. Harmony. Important choices.*

The Lovers

POSITIVE

There are a few ideas to be taken into consideration when the Lovers card appears and the first of these is that love may indeed be on the way. If you are lonely, there will soon be someone around for you to love, and if you simply need a bit of company and companionship, this too is around the corner. The atmosphere amongst your workmates, friends and family will be peaceful and harmonious in the future and your surroundings will become nicer and more attractive. A relationship that is in its infancy will become stronger and if you have any doubts about the sincerity of your lover, then this card is a reassuring one to find.

The second main idea is that of choices to be made and you are reminded that your decisions will have a ripple effect on those around you. Therefore, if you choose to embark on a new romance, start a course of training or to take a job in a new location, the needs of your loved ones must be taken into account.

NEGATIVE

This card suggests that a current or future love affair will go nowhere and that a fling will be short lived. On the other hand, you could lose out by keeping your real feelings to yourself and by playing things a little too coolly. You could be on the point of making the wrong choice or of making a complete idiot of yourself. Worse still, you may soon settle for someone who will not be good to you. Take care with all your choices and decisions now because their effect on others may be harmful.

The Chariot

Number: 7

Key ideas: *Travel and transport.*
Conflict and battles that will be won.

The Chariot

POSITIVE

The Chariot is a card of movement, so an important journey or a number of future trips for business or pleasure are in the pipeline. Sometimes this card shows that you will soon buy or replace a vehicle. A time of struggle and effort is in the cards, but the outcome will be worthwhile. You may take on a large task such as moving house or tackling a big job soon but although there is a lot involved, it will be for the best in the long run. If you are suddenly faced with difficulties or opposition, the advice is not to back away from the situation but to face it and fight it.

You will feel as though your particular chariot is being drawn by two very different horses because doubt, uncertainty and conflicting demands will plague you for a while.

NEGATIVE

This card means much the same whether upright or reversed or whether surrounded by good or bad cards. A battle must be fought and it may take a while before you overcome your problems. There could be difficulties related to travel and transport in the near future. Another negative feature may be doubtfulness so it would be a good idea to think through any proposed course of action from all the angles and then either leave it alone or go for it with all your heart.

Strength

Number: 8

Key ideas: *Endurance.*
Tact and diplomacy. Health and strength.

8

Strength

POSITIVE

The image on this card is of a young woman gently closing a lion's mouth. The strength card is often described as depicting the female forces of endurance, perseverance and patience rather than raw masculine energy. The message is to keep going through a difficult situation instead of running away from it. This does not suggest that you should put up with being bullied, but on the contrary, quietly and courageously stand up to tyranny. Truth and light will overcome spite and jealousy. This card advises that tact and diplomacy will be of more use than losing your temper. If you have been sick in mind, body or spirit, you will soon recover and if a loved one is sick, the same thing applies.

NEGATIVE

The news here is that a sick person has still got some way to go before recovery. A struggle will prove too difficult or a situation can't or shouldn't be endured any longer.

The Hermit

Number: 9

Key ideas: *Retreat and reflection.*
A light dawns.

The Hermit

POSITIVE

The figure on this card is of an old man who is
holding a long staff and carrying a lamp. He is
alone. This card promises a period of time away
from the hustle and bustle of daily life and it
suggests that you need to do some quiet thinking,
and to come to a few sensible conclusions. For
those who are spiritually inclined, prayer and
meditation bring enlightenment and spiritual guidance. The Hermit can also
indicate a period spent quietly studying or researching.

You may feel alone and lonely, even if you are surrounded by a family or a
whole horde of work colleagues. A counsellor, a wise friend or an older and
wiser person will turn up if you need one, but the main message is to accept
restriction as it will benefit you in the long run.

NEGATIVE

There are a number of interpretations to be found here. You could resent having
to be alone or you could turn away from those who want to help you, maybe
slamming the door on others and then bemoaning your fate. Alternatively, you
may fail to grow up and see things as they are. Lastly, you may be suffering
from a bereavement or the loss of a lover. In the case of the latter, the lover will
not come back and you will spend some time alone getting over things. Positive
or negative, this is one of life's lessons and the experience will make you wiser
(and older).

Wheel of Fortune

Number: 10

Key ideas: *Change.*

Wheel of Fortune

POSITIVE

This card has only one meaning and that is simply
that the Wheel of Fortune is about to turn,
bringing changes of circumstances. The images on
the card are of the four fixed signs of the zodiac
(Taurus, Leo, Scorpio and Aquarius) which signify
stability, but in this case, the stability will
temporarily disappear from your life. The fixed
signs can also denote the four corners of the world,
so travel or a new horizon of a metaphorical kind is likely in the near future.
Some consultants take this card to mean that good fortune is on the way, but in
reality this card is neither good nor bad; it simply means that fate is about to
take a hand in your life.

NEGATIVE

This may simply mean that the changes you crave are still a little way off in the
future or alternatively, that the change will come but not in the way you might
choose or expect.

Justice

Number: 11

Key ideas: *Justice and fair play.*
Legal matters. Balance.

POSITIVE

The Justice card shows a female figure holding a
sword and the scales of justice. It means that
justice will prevail and the outcome of a dispute will
be fair to all concerned. If you have been unfairly
treated, an apology will be forthcoming, but if you
have been hard on someone else, it may be you
that has to do the apologizing. If you have

Justice

documents to sign or legal matters to attend to, these things will soon be
resolved to your satisfaction.

   The second meaning is that if your life has been a little one-sided recently,
the balance will soon be re-established.

NEGATIVE

You will continue to be treated unfairly for a while longer and, indeed, you may
never get a satisfactory result. If you have any legal matters to deal with, ensure
that you have the right advisor and that you read all the small print on any
document. If you are considering bringing a case against another person, be
aware that you can win or lose.

The Hanged Man

Number: 12

Key ideas: *Sacrifice. Initiation.*
Suspension. Waiting.

POSITIVE

The image on this card is of a man hanging by
his foot from a wooden frame. He doesn't look
unhappy or even uncomfortable in this position.
The card suggests that in order to have something
that you want, something else will have to be
sacrificed, as the two items are not compatible.
A typical idea would be to sacrifice security for
freedom and vice versa. You may simply have to give something up for no
reason at all.

The concept of initiation is that you can never understand a particular set of
circumstances unless you go through what others have gone through. Sadness,
loss, fear, worry, and negative emotions and experiences are a normal part of
life and when any of these rotten events come to pass, you will learn something
from them. Finally, if you are waiting to hear about something or to get
something off the ground, the Hanged Man suggests that this will be held up
for a while longer.

NEGATIVE

Don't make useless sacrifices or wait indefinitely for something that is not going
to come your way. Leave it alone and do something else.

Death

Number: 13

Key ideas: *The end of a situation.*
Transformation.

Death

POSITIVE

The ghastly figure of a skeleton on a horse
frightens newcomers to the Tarot because they
think that this signifies their imminent departure
from this world. This is not so, because the card
simply denotes that something is going to come to
an end and in many cases, this is a very good
thing. An unpleasant job, unsatisfactory
relationship or even an illness will come to an end, allowing for new
developments to come along. This card can mean that someone around you is
coming to the end of their life or that you will hear of a death, but its usual
meaning is of an ending and a subsequent change of circumstances.

NEGATIVE

This card means much the same either way up, but if you are particularly keen
to have something come to an end, a reversed Death card suggests that this will
take longer than you think.

Temperance

Number: 14

Key idea: *Moderation in all things. Peace.*

14

Temperance

POSITIVE

There are times in everyone's life when things work out well and when everything runs smoothly. This card suggests that just such a time is on the way to you. The Temperance card shows a young woman pouring liquid from one vessel to another, suggesting the mixture of ingredients into just the right potion. You may not have as much money to play with as you would wish, which means that you will need to temper your future spending. However, a time of peace and relaxation is on the way.

NEGATIVE

You have too much going on in your life and you should cut back on some of your activities or your spending.

The Devil

Number: 15

Key ideas: *Bondage. Responsibilities. Guilt. Bad influences.*

The Devil

POSITIVE

This ugly card upsets those who are unfamiliar with the Tarot as they expect it to mean that evil things are coming their way. The main idea here is of bondage and this can take many forms. You may quite sensibly take on a large responsibility, such as a mortgage or an obligation, or you may mortgage your free time by starting a course of education. These matters are positive, but they still tie you down.

More positively, this card can indicate a good sexual relationship to come!

NEGATIVE

Negatively, there are a whole host of things than can tie you in knots and these may range from debts, unnecessary feelings of guilt, a lousy relationship, a job or a business that isn't viable, a terrible family life and much more. There may be people who would love to see you hooked on just about anything that gives them control over you. Your own negative feelings can exert an even stronger form of bondage. Beware of jealousy towards you or your own jealous feelings.

If you are being held back by any of the aforementioned ideas, you will soon free yourself and spiritual enlightenment is on the way.

The Tower

Number: 16

Key ideas: *A shock or upheaval.*
Problems with property or premises.

The Tower

POSITIVE

The Tower card shows a building that is burning
and people falling from the windows. This
terrifying image suggests that your world is about
to be turned upside down. The shock or upheaval
that the Tower predicts may not turn out to be a
major disaster but you can be sure that something
unpleasant will occur. Often this discovery is a
blessing in disguise because it means that something you are unaware of comes
to light, and it is better to know what is going on than to be kept in the dark.

Experience has taught me that the Tower card can warn of trouble related
to property or premises, so when this card shows up, look up your local
handyman's phone number!

NEGATIVE

A nasty surprise is on the way and although unpleasant, it is not disastrous and
can be dealt with fairly quickly. You may already be aware of the problem. A
minor household problem will irritate you. Be prepared to call out a plumber
or a builder.

The Star

Number: 17

Key ideas: *Hope. A bright future. Optimism.*

The Star

POSITIVE

The star card shows a young girl pouring one jug of water on to the land and another into a pond or stream and in the sky above her head, several bright stars are shining. The Star predicts hope for the future and good things to look forward to. The notion is that the stars and planets in your horoscope will soon be in a beneficial alignment and that the future is bright. This is an excellent card to draw if you are hoping to study any subject, but astrological or spiritual studies would be especially well favoured.

NEGATIVE

This card is excellent whichever way it falls, but you may have to wait a while before your wish is granted. The only other warning is not to waste your talents or your energies by pouring half of them into the wrong receptacle.

The Moon

Number: 18

Key ideas: *Unclear vision. Muddles and mysteries. Deception. Emotionalism.*

The Moon

POSITIVE

The Moon card shows a moonlit scene with a road emerging from a lake and winding into a mysterious distance, between two apparently pointless towers that are perched on a hill. A dog, a jackal and a weird crustacean are shown too. The mysterious nature of this card exactly fits the muddled and deceptive turn of events that surrounds you.

I have often seen this card emerge when a client is in an emotional mess. One typical scenario is that you are being lied to and deceived by a lover. Alternatively, it could mean that you yourself are involved with more than one person and don't know what to do about it. You can't trust anyone when this card appears, and your own feelings are confusing and frightening. In business, financial or legal matters, this card offers a warning to proceed with extreme caution. If your intuition tells you that things are not all they seem to be, listen to this inner voice. You don't know the whole story—still less what is really in the minds of those around you—and there are matters that have yet to be revealed to you.

Finally, this card can denote a trip that is taken to a cool or wet place and if so, the journey itself will be strange and unusual.

NEGATIVE

The Moon card means much the same either way up, but this may show that the problem won't go away just yet.

The Sun

Number: 19

Key ideas: *Success. Joy and happiness. A child enters your circle.*

The Sun

POSITIVE

The Sun card shows a child, flowers and a large and happy sun shining down, and it means that success and happiness are on the way. Exams will be passed, and tribulations overcome. If you are entering a new love relationship, this will be happy and successful. A happy marriage could be in the pipeline, and whatever you are wishing for will work out just the way you want. If you have been ill or simply fed up, you will soon be feeling much better.

In some cases, this card suggests that a baby is on the way or that a child will become important to you. In other cases, this card suggests that the summer will be a particularly happy time or perhaps that a holiday in the sun would do you the world of good.

NEGATIVE

There is nothing negative about this card, but if it is reversed in a spread, it can mean that you will have to wait a little longer than you would like for the happiness you seek.

Judgement

Number: 20

Key ideas: *The end of a phase. Legal judgement. Something coming back to life.*

20

Judgement

POSITIVE

The illustration on the Judgement card depicts the day of judgement when souls rise out of the grave to be judged. On a spiritual wavelength, this implies that one particular phase of your soul's journey is at an end, and you will shortly assess what you learned and how you coped with the passing situation. Much the same can be said of practical matters because something is ending and you will soon sum up its value to you. Whether you have been given a retirement present, a certificate of achievement or whether you have simply survived a particularly difficult or even a particularly good phase in life, the idea here is to look back and see what was learned and to judge your performance.

A second meaning is that an idea that has been shelved will now come back to life again, allowing you to judge its worth and to take it up if you still wish to. Lastly, if there is a legal matter yet to be settled, it soon will be.

NEGATIVE

The negative version of this card denotes dissatisfaction with the outcome of a project or a phase of life. You may be displeased because you didn't try hard enough or because the project just didn't work. There are lessons to be learned here, but nevertheless, it is time to move on and try something else. If legal matters are in the air, this is a warning that they may not work out to your satisfaction.

The World

Number: 21

Key ideas: *Completion. Full circle.*

21

The World

POSITIVE

The World card shows an attractive dancer
holding two staffs of office; she is surrounded by a
wreath. The fixed signs of the zodiac in the four
corners of the card suggest the four corners of the
earth. This card means that a phase of life is at an
end and that the circle is completed. It rarely
suggests a sudden ending, rather a natural
progression, a graceful turning point and a time to
put the past behind you and to move on to fresh fields and pastures. In a
spiritual context, the card tells you that even life itself is not finite, because
reincarnation means a movement on to a new spiritual level. Whatever
circumstances the World card refers to, it is a satisfactory card to find because
it simply means that the job is done and that it is time to move on. Sometimes
travel, new vistas and expansion of horizons are indicated.

NEGATIVE

If reversed, the World card can imply that you won't be happy to see this
particular phase of your life coming to an end. In other cases, the ending in
question can't come fast enough for you and that, indeed, it is still some way
off into the future.

THE MINOR ARCANA
The Suit of Wands

Wand cards belong to the element of fire and may be attributed to the astrological signs of Aries, Leo and Sagittarius. Wand cards imply enthusiasm and optimism and refer to normal day-to-day matters, especially communication, negotiation and business. Whether they concern your career or your private life, travel or movement in affairs are indicated. Wand cards may refer to buying, selling or renting property.

Ace of Wands

POSITIVE

All aces suggest new beginnings but this one specifically suggests a rebirth, a time to emerge and do something new and exciting. If you are waiting for news, especially in connection with business, it is on the way and the news will be good. There may be a child on the way in your family circle or a creative venture to get off the ground.

NEGATIVE

The news you are waiting for will be delayed or maybe not as good as you would hope. A new beginning brings problems. Perhaps the idea is right, but the timing is wrong.

Ace of Wands

Two of Wands

POSITIVE

There will be a successful partnership or joint venture in the near future. This card is an excellent one for property dealings, especially if a lover or partner is involved. The two can mean that you should hang on to money or keep a job going in one place, while using some of your resources for a new and expansive project elsewhere. A proud man may soon enter your life.

NEGATIVE

Delays in business or property matters. Travel is best left for another time. Partnership deals are problematic and a proud or vain man may be the cause of the problem.

Three of Wands

POSITIVE

This card brings fresh enterprises and something new to enquire about. Negotiations will go well and there may be an exciting new job to take up. Travel in connection with work is favoured and correspondence or phone calls will bring good news. Marriage or business partnerships are favoured.

NEGATIVE

Business matters will be delayed or problematic. Try again later.

Four of Wands

POSITIVE

You will soon put down roots in a comfortable environment and if you are hoping to buy or sell property, this card brings good news. A holiday will be a success.

NEGATIVE

Moves may be delayed or surrounded by problems. If you visit friends or relatives, keep the visit short and don't spend your whole holiday in their home.

Five of Wands

POSITIVE

There will be plenty of work and you will enjoy the challenge. You will struggle to get what you want, but even this is enjoyable and the outcome will be worth it. Travel plans may have to be put back because you will be too busy to get away.

NEGATIVE

There may be legal or other difficulties ahead. Don't take on a difficult task now if you can avoid it.

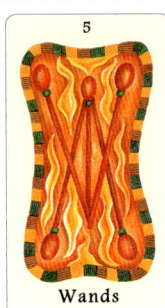

Six of Wands

POSITIVE

This card is often referred to as the card of victory as it depicts a victor coming home after a battle. Your particular battle may relate to business and finances, a legal matter, studying and examinations.

NEGATIVE

Those whom you depend upon will let you down and you must not leave others to do your job for you. If you can avoid a battle or a struggle now, do so, because the outcome won't please you.

Seven of Wands

POSITIVE

A sensible approach will allow you to cope with anything. Divide a job up into pieces rather than tackle the whole thing head on. You will face opposition or you may have to work while feeling ill. The message is to keep going, take things step by step and not to give up.

NEGATIVE

There will be too many problems around you, so tackle only what is important. Don't take the responsibilities or problems of others on your back and refrain from interfering in the lives of others. Leave chancy decisions for another time.

Eight of Wands

POSITIVE

This is a card of expansion and it often signifies travel. New faces and new experiences are on the way, and there will be friendship and maybe even love in the near future.

NEGATIVE

Plans will be cancelled, possibly even by strike action! Stay close to home and on familiar ground. There may be jealousy and spite around you or you may have reason to feel envy in the future.

Nine of Wands

POSITIVE

This suggests that your situation will be secure, but it may be slightly restricting. There should be little to trouble you apart from the fact that others will make demands upon your time. Most of your problems will soon be behind you.

NEGATIVE

A loss of status and position are possible. Illness may be on the way.

Ten of Wands

POSITIVE

Burdens will be placed upon you and you will have your hands full. A task will require patience, endurance and strength, but there is nothing to suppose that you can't or won't get through it. Success can be achieved, but it will take hard work before you reach your goal.

NEGATIVE

Burdens and responsibilities will shortly ease. If you are looking for promotion or if you want to tackle a large or long-winded job, leave this for the time being.

Page of Wands

POSITIVE

Pages can refer to young people and, as such, this is a bright and lively youngster who is intelligent, charming and talkative. Sometimes, this signifies the arrival of young visitors or a new baby.

The Page of Wands suggests that letters, phone calls, and good news are on the way. News from old friends or business news will be good. Minor property matters will be successful. If you want to write for a living, this is an excellent indication of future success.

NEGATIVE

A young person will be troubled and he or she may cause you trouble. Travel, contracts and negotiations will be held up.

Page of Wands

Knight of Wands

POSITIVE

The Knight in question is likely to be a young male, but don't be too dogmatic about the age group (or gender) when dealing with this card. The Knight suggests that a pleasant, talkative, intelligent person is about to make a contribution to your life. This person enhances your love life, business life or social life.

All Knight cards promise movement and this one suggests travel or even a change of address.

NEGATIVE

A man will let you down. He may be full of big talk or promises that turn out to be worthless. Travel will be disappointing and visitors may change their mind about visiting you. There will be difficulties in relation to property or money matters. Don't bank on anything just yet.

Knight of Wands

Queen of Wands

POSITIVE

This card represents a charming and clever woman who is a good companion. She is an excellent and very ethical businesswoman who uses communication skills in her work. This lady is reliable in matters of love, but she cannot be tied down or bossed around. She makes a great friend or a sexy lover.

As a situation, this suggests an upturn in business matters with some travel involved. A businesswoman will advise and help you.

NEGATIVE

Either this lady is unreliable or she is well-meaning, but unable to help at the moment.

Queen of Wands

King of Wands

POSITIVE

This man of mature years is a good communicator and listener. He has a sense of humour and he is a good conversationalist, but he may be shy with new people. Honest and intelligent, he would make an excellent work colleague. As a lover, he is good company and he will cheer you up.

As a situation, this suggests an upturn in business and there is a possibility of travel or of liaising with others on a project.

NEGATIVE

As a man, this person cannot be relied upon. He may be a liar and apt to make promises that he won't keep, and in business and love he will prove disappointing. In some cases, the man is all right, but he is otherwise involved or in a poor position to give you what you need.

King of Wands

The Suit of Pentacles

Pentacle cards belong to the element of earth and they can be associated with the astrological signs of Taurus, Virgo and Capricorn. Pentacles refer to money, resources, goods and services, the organization of work, business, and one's status. Property and large purchases also come under the rule of the Pentacles. Gains and losses involving money, goods, and tangible assets are indicated. Tarot cards always advise against greed, materialism, or selfishness, so be generous to others when you can.

Ace of Pentacles

POSITIVE

All Aces refer to the start of something and in the case of the Pentacle, this shows that your finances are about to improve. There will be a new source of income or some additional cash. You may win something, have a windfall or receive a letter bringing good news about money.

NEGATIVE

This is much the same as the positive reading, but the financial improvement may not be all that great. Alternatively, the money you need will come along a little later than you would like.

Ace of Pentacles

Two of Pentacles

POSITIVE

At best there will be enough money coming in to cover your outgoings, but there won't be much left over. You will have to juggle your funds for a while longer. In some cases, this card foretells a separation of resources, possibly due to a divorce or the break-up of a partnership. There will be more demands upon you than you have time and energy to cope with.

NEGATIVE

This card is much the same either way up, but there is a definite warning here not to gamble or be reckless with money.

Three of Pentacles

POSITIVE

A decent and well-paid job may be offered to you but I often find this card is also linked to property matters. In many cases it talks of both these situations, because an increase in earnings helps you to improve your home or to find a better place to live.

NEGATIVE

The reversed or negative meaning is much the same as above, but there may be delays or problems surrounding your career, or there may be difficulties associated with work that you choose to have done on your home.

Four of Pentacles

POSITIVE

Financial security is on the way, both in the short term and long term, but you must guard against becoming materialistic, greedy or smug about your good fortune.

NEGATIVE

A cash-flow problem will arise and money will be tight for a while, but you can find outlets that don't require much money.

Five of Pentacles

POSITIVE

There is danger of financial loss and hardship, but in many cases this relates more to fear of loss than actual loss. You may be looking for security in the wrong place. This card can bring fun in connection with flirtations and light-hearted affairs.

NEGATIVE

With a bit of luck and a sensible attitude, loss and loneliness will end soon. However, if a greedy or stupid attitude over money prevails, you will lose more than you can afford.

Six of Pentacles

POSITIVE

This card indicates paying out money or clearing debts or obligations to others. If you have borrowed money or goods, you will shortly be in a position to repay your benefactors. You may receive a payment or the return of a favour from someone else. The sharing out can come as a result of a divorce or a business split. You will help those who are in need.

NEGATIVE

Debts and shortage of funds continue for a while longer. Don't be persuaded to give away more than you can afford.

Seven of Pentacles

POSITIVE

You will get where you want to be in the end. If your job is arduous or if you are getting a business of your own off the ground, this will be successful, but it will take time. Your financial situation is improving. Don't give up.

NEGATIVE

A period of hard work will come to an end or, alternatively, you could come to the conclusion that what you are doing isn't worth the effort it takes. Not the right time to take on a large task.

Eight of Pentacles

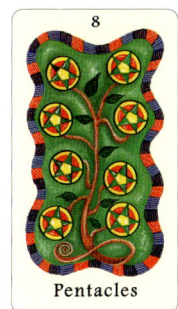

8

Pentacles

POSITIVE
This is an excellent card if you are looking for a new job or for a step up in a current one. The same goes if you want to start or improve a business or even to embark on a big task around the home. Hard work brings success, rewards and satisfaction.

NEGATIVE
There may be problems at work and your present job may come to an end. Promotion will elude you. You need to learn new skills and techniques. In some cases, the news is good, but it will take time for you to achieve the success you seek.

Nine of Pentacles

9

Pentacles

POSITIVE
Money, success and abundance are on the way. If you want a new address in a better location or if you want to buy attractive goods for your home, the outlook is good. Your financial situation will change for the better.

NEGATIVE
Financial difficulties will continue for a while longer and it may take time before you can find the home that you want. In some cases, this card simply means that it is time to have a clear-out prior to moving or refurbishing a home.

Ten of Pentacles

10

Pentacles

POSITIVE
This card brings money, success, resources, and security for the future. It indicates financial and emotional security. The old-fashioned meaning of this card is the start of a dynasty, implying that whatever you start now will stand the test of time.

NEGATIVE
Success and money are on the way, but this won't be earth-shattering. There may be a gift or a windfall on the way.

Page of Pentacles

POSITIVE

Page cards sometimes talk about children and young people and in this case the youngster is quiet, serious and businesslike. If applicable, there would be good news for or about a youngster.

Otherwise, this card brings news about money, business or travel in connection with work. It can indicate a raise in pay or promotion at work. A small increase in finances is on the way.

NEGATIVE

There may be a slight problem for a youngster who is around you or, alternatively, business or financial matters will be slightly disappointing.

Page of Pentacles

Knight of Pentacles

POSITIVE

Knights are usually considered to be youngish men, but it is best not to be dogmatic about age or gender. This person is cautious and money-minded. A man brings news about business, money or travel in connection with business. As a lover, this man is sincere, reliable and decent, but materialistic.

Otherwise this card brings good news about work, money and travel in connection with financial matters. Steady progress can be made.

NEGATIVE

A man may cost you money or let you down over a business matter. Otherwise, problems connected with work, business travel and finances may arise.

Knight of Pentacles

Queen of Pentacles

POSITIVE

As a person, this signifies a good business woman who is honest, reliable, and a skilled negotiator. She is a high-maintenance lady who needs a good standard of living, and if she cannot get it through marriage or some other means, she will make money for herself.

NEGATIVE

A woman may be too money-minded and she may try to take more than her fair share of goods, time or energy from you. As a situation, this shows that some extra expense will be incurred but that there is still a chance of improving your situation.

Queen of Pentacles

King of Pentacles

POSITIVE

This is a strong business-like man who is in a position to help and advise you. He may be your accountant or bank-manager. This conservative businessman is honest and a little tough in his dealings and, while he is a little too materialistic, he is also a good family man who can be relied upon.

NEGATIVE

This money-minded man may try to take you for all that he can get. He may appear steady and reliable, but in reality he is a poor advisor, a loser or perhaps temporarily down on his luck. In personal matters, this guy can be stingy or a bully. Otherwise, a slight financial setback may befall you.

King of Pentacles

The Suit of Cups

Cup cards are associated with the element of water and the zodiac signs of Cancer, Scorpio and Pisces. This suit is concerned with love, emotion, affection, friendship, creativity, and how you feel about anyone or anything. For example, you may love your home or hate your job. Cups talk about love relationships of every sort, including long-standing marriages, romantic attachments or short-lived affairs. They can be associated with creative projects that you feel deeply about, so when these cards appear, stop and consider what it is that they are actually referring to.

Ace of Cups

POSITIVE

Aces all represent new beginnings and this card can indicate the start of a love affair and an outpouring of emotion. This may represent the way someone is going to feel about you or how you will feel about someone else. If a creative venture is on your mind, this is a very positive card to draw.

NEGATIVE

This card can indicate that a lover is losing interest or that there is affection to be had, but not the all-embracing love that you seek. Perhaps the love is there, but muddles and confusion abound.

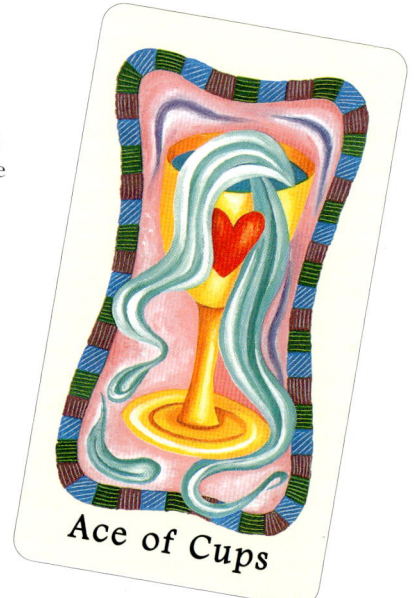

Ace of Cups

Two of Cups

POSITIVE

A partnership or a love affair is on the way and in either case this will be very pleasant and a great success. If you have quarrelled with a lover or a friend, you will soon make up.

NEGATIVE

A parting or a separation may be permanent or temporary. An affair may not get off the ground. Guard against loving someone who doesn't return your love.

Three of Cups

POSITIVE

A celebration will take place. This may be a wedding, the birth of a child, a house-warming, a business success or anything else that gives you a reason to celebrate. A woman's club or a group of female friends brings fun and support.

NEGATIVE

You may have a brief affair or something else that gives you short-lived or half-hearted joy. You may decide against a marriage or partnership, or you may split from a current partner.

Four of Cups

POSITIVE

Despite the fact that you will have most of what you want from life, you will still feel that something is missing. Maybe the practicalities of your situation will be great, but the romance lacking. Perhaps you just want more of everything.

NEGATIVE

You begin to accept the limitations of your situation and as a result you relax and enjoy life more. New friends and new experiences are on the way.

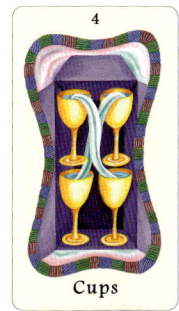

Five of Cups

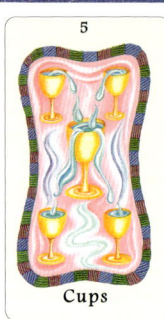

POSITIVE

This is a sad card that foretells an emotional loss or sadness. It may be that a relationship doesn't bring all that you would wish, or you may part company from someone you love. All is not lost as other factors will compensate.

NEGATIVE

A period of sadness or unhappiness passes and there will be happiness for you in the future. You will meet up with old friends and make some new ones.

Six of Cups

POSITIVE

This is a nostalgic card for good times past. A family gathering brings you back into contact with people you like and it is possible that an old flame may re-enter your life. You will find old skills and old contacts invaluable.

NEGATIVE

This is no time to look backwards as the past is now past, and it is time to move forward in business and in your personal life. If friends vanish, they will make way for new ones to come.

Seven of Cups

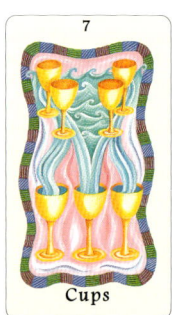

POSITIVE

You have many options open to you and many paths to choose from, and this makes it hard for you to know exactly which way to go. Wait a while to see which turns out to be the best and, if in doubt, use your intuition or tune into your spiritual guides for help. If money has been a stumbling block to romance, this will sort itself out.

NEGATIVE

A time of muddle is ending and the future is beginning to look much clearer.

Eight of Cups

POSITIVE

This sad card shows that you have some way to go before you can move to a happier situation. If you have been hurt by a lover you must put this behind you, write it off to experience, and move on. Your misery will soon end, and with fortitude, you will find happiness again. An old gypsy reading is that a fair-haired woman will help you out and, oddly enough, I have found this interpretation to be accurate.

NEGATIVE

A rotten situation comes to an end and there will be fun and joy in the future.

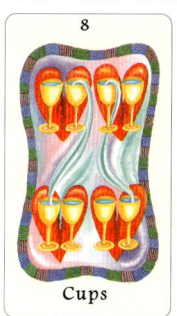

Nine of Cups

POSITIVE

Some call this the wish card as it appears to fulfil all your wishes. This card shows that you will soon be satisfied with life, but it warns against smugness or boastfulness.

NEGATIVE

You may need to make one more effort to achieve your ambitions. For example, if you fail an exam you should re-take it as you will pass it the second time. Life may be mildly irritating but your problems will soon be behind you.

Ten of Cups

POSITIVE

Happiness, joy, and love are yours for the taking. Family life will be happy, secure, and satisfying.

NEGATIVE

Don't allow someone else to spoil your happiness or to cause disruptions in your family. Don't allow others to take the credit for your achievements or to interfere. If you prevent these difficulties from occurring, your future life should be good.

Page of Cups

POSITIVE

Pages can be interpreted as children and young people, and the Page of Cups represents an artistic or creative youngster who is attractive and gentle. In some cases, this denotes the arrival of a new baby in the family.

Otherwise, this card suggests a period of training or study and that your studies will be spiritual or creative in nature. Business matters need thought and nothing should be rushed into.

NEGATIVE

A sensitive youngster will present you with a problem. If you are studying, you will hit a difficult patch or you will be short of time.

Page of Cups

Knight of Cups

POSITIVE

Knights are considered to be youngish men, but the age and even the gender are flexible. The Knight of Cups is a kindly and pleasant person who is a good advisor and friend. He is gentle, soft-hearted, and great company. He is stylish and he has an eye for beauty and value, but if you want someone to lean on, this person may be too weak.

NEGATIVE

This Knight is lazy, weak, selfish and unreliable. He will travel or move away from you as soon as you begin to make demands upon him. He needs an easy, stress-free life.

Knight of Cups

Queen of Cups

POSITIVE

This mature lady is warm-hearted, kind and very feminine. She is artistic and a good home-maker, but she is surprisingly materialistic and she cannot live without a good standard of living. Generally speaking, this is not a career woman. This Queen makes a good friend and a pleasant lover, but she needs to be looked after.

NEGATIVE

This lady can be weak, self-indulgent and lazy. She may be looking for a meal ticket or someone to take responsibility from her shoulders.

Queen of Cups

King of Cups

POSITIVE

This mature man is pleasant, kind and warm-hearted. He may not be terribly generous, but he makes a good advisor and a pleasing friend. In love, he can be romantic and sexy, but he may not be as strong or as reliable as you would wish and he can be surprisingly possessive. He is a canny but somewhat lazy businessman.

NEGATIVE

This King can be selfish, greedy and weak. He may promise much, but he won't fulfil all that he promises. He is unreliable in business or in romance, but this may simply be due to his current circumstances rather than his nature.

King of Cups

The Suit of Swords

Sword cards are associated with the element of air and the zodiac signs of Gemini, Libra and Aquarius, and indicate new ideas and intellectual growth. Swords appear when action needs to be taken and when illness, troubles, or a battle of some kind has to be faced up to. Most of all, swords denote the need to be decisive, suggesting that we cannot avoid trouble, but must tackle problems promptly, with the aid of professional help if necessary. If action isn't taken, the cards denote entrapment and suffering. Lawyers, doctors and financial advisors are often indicated by the Swords.

Ace of Swords

Ace of Swords

POSITIVE

All Aces signify a new start and in this case new ideas and projects are likely. You will soon take control of a situation, make decisions and make things happen. If you have been treated unjustly, this will be rectified. You will have to speak out, but you must avoid throwing your weight around. This Ace can indicate a medical or dental problem that will be solved by surgery.

NEGATIVE

The reversed or negative reading is much the same as above, although perhaps milder in its effects. You must avoid going too far or being too critical of others.

Two of Swords

POSITIVE

A stalemate situation exists and this applies to those of you who desperately want things to change, just as much as to those who are keen for things to remain as they are. A peace treaty, an apology or a settlement will occur soon, but nothing will really change.

NEGATIVE

A stalemate situation is coming to an end. Someone may travel away soon and this will bring a feeling of relief and release.

Three of Swords

POSITIVE

There will be losses, heartache and sadness, and possible rejection to be faced. An illness is indicated for you or for someone around you and this could take the form of heart trouble or even of an operation in the near future.

NEGATIVE

An end of heartache is in sight and you will come to terms with loss or rejection. A minor surgical procedure is possible, as is going to a funeral.

Four of Swords

POSITIVE

If you have been ill, you will recover soon and if you have been overdoing things, you will be able to rest and relax. There will be a time of rest after a battle. If a loved one is sick, they will recover soon.

NEGATIVE

Whether you have to fight to achieve something or if your fight is against illness, it will take time for this to be resolved.

Five of Swords

POSITIVE

There will be quarrels and possibly even violence! You can't back away from a fight and you must stand up for what you believe in, even if it means parting company from someone close to you. If a close associate wishes to get on with his/her life and to move out of your orbit, don't stop them.

NEGATIVE

This is similar to the reading above, but it indicates that the storm clouds are passing away. You may go to a funeral soon.

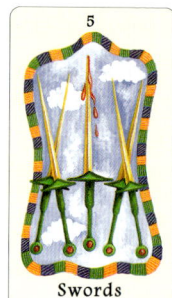

Swords

Six of Swords

POSITIVE

Travel, crossing water, moving from one place to another and even a holiday in a cool place are indicated here. In some cases, the movement is metaphoric in that you stay where you are, but move on mentally or emotionally. There may be visits from distant friends or relatives.

NEGATIVE

Travel delays or disappointments, also losses due to carelessness.

Swords

Seven of Swords

POSITIVE

Watch out for robbers and swindlers. You will soon move into a new environment, leaving something or someone behind, while taking with you what you will need for your future circumstances.

NEGATIVE

Two meanings here: the first being to look out for thieves; the second being to take legal or financial advice before taking any important steps.

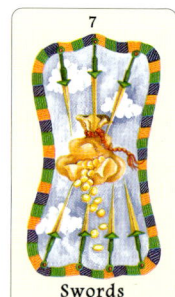

Swords

Eight of Swords

POSITIVE

For some people this card indicates a spell in prison! More likely, you will feel tied down and unable to break out and make changes. The odd thing is that you may well be able to make the break, but you lack the strength or the courage to do so. You may not have enough reason (or enough money) to leave a current situation.

NEGATIVE

Restrictions will lift, but depression, difficulties and maybe a battle will have to be fought first. There may be illness, accidents, a prison sentence or even a death in your circle.

Nine of Swords

POSITIVE

This is a classic card of sleepless nights and worry, and I have often found it to relate to a mother worrying about her children. Sometimes the problem is in the sufferer's mind and is not actually as bad as it seems.

NEGATIVE

Worry and sleeplessness will pass. Someone may spread rumours about you.

Ten of Swords

POSITIVE

Someone will stab you in the back or let you down badly. A project is problematic. There may be treachery, a divorce, a business collapse or some other disaster on the way. Changes are inevitable whether you want them or not.

NEGATIVE

Minor disappointments and people who cannot fulfil all that they promise to you. Hard times are coming to an end and recovery from illness is promised.

Page of Swords

POSITIVE

Pages are often children or young people, and in this case the youngster is intelligent, quick and probably sporty.

As a situation, you are being advised to keep your eyes open and to listen to any tips that your friends come up with. A contract or important legal document will benefit you.

NEGATIVE

An intelligent but difficult young person may make your life tough for a while. Beware of those who gossip behind the backs of others or whose intentions are malicious. Contracts and legal documents must be looked at carefully.

Page of Swords

Knight of Swords

POSITIVE

Knights are usually youngish men, but the age and the gender can be flexible. In this case, the person is tough, courageous and intelligent. The Knight will rush into your life and while he may not actually become a major factor or a long-term partner, he will have a catalytic effect.

As a situation, this indicates a time of action with travel being a strong possibility. You will have to think quickly, but avoid making wrong decisions due to haste.

NEGATIVE

A sarcastic, chaotic, or even violent man may enter your life now. Guard against being sucked into criminal or self-destructive behaviour.

Knight of Swords

Queen of Swords

POSITIVE

This is a mature woman who is intelligent and in command of her circumstances, but her sharp tongue makes enemies for her. She may be an excellent professional or personal advisor and in some cases a good friend. This woman may be a widow, divorcee or simply alone by choice.

As a situation, the advice is to think clearly and to take courageous decisions.

NEGATIVE

A sharp, unpleasant and hurtful person who may be an adversary in your business or personal life. This lady can be cruel and malicious.

Queen of Swords

King of Swords

POSITIVE

This mature man is intelligent and knowledgeable, but he can be cold-hearted. If you need professional advice, there is no one better. As a lover, this man is too logical, cool and unfeeling to live with for long, but as a work colleague—especially in the fields of science or research—he is dependable. If you need a doctor or a lawyer, this is a good card to draw.

NEGATIVE

This man can be a nasty piece of work or he may simply be working against you, and this is especially so if you are involved in any kind of legal battle. This man will use his intelligence against you and he may take money from you or otherwise let you down. If you need a doctor or other professional person, make sure the one you choose is competent. Take care.

King of Swords

TAROT NUMBERS

Aces

Aces signify the start of something new, which may result from a stroke of fate or a personal decision.

Ace of Wands

Ace of Cups

Ace of Swords

Ace of Pentacles

Twos

Twos refer to relating with others and this may be in business or personal life.

2 Wands

2 Cups

2 Swords

2 Pentacles

Threes

Threes denote creative new enterprises or losses, and these often involve others as well as yourself.

3 Wands

3 Cups

3 Swords

3 Pentacles

Fours

Fours bring safety, security and relief from problems.

4 Wands

4 Swords

4 Cups

4 Pentacles

Fives

Fives all denote challenges which may be desired or result from loss.

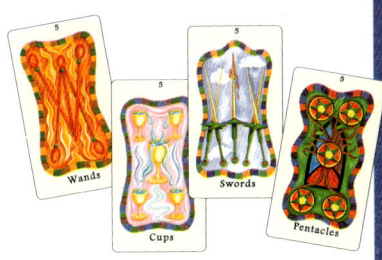

Sixes

Sixes suggest conclusions to minor matters, also useful turning points.

Sevens

Sevens signify some confusion and decisions based on the reality of a situation.

Eights

Eights characterize freedom and restriction, plus decisions that need action.

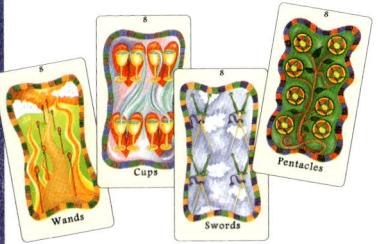

Nines

Nines show situations that are either comfortable or uncomfortable.

Tens

Tens mean that the outcome of a situation will be either a complete success or an utter failure.

Pages

Pages can represent children or young people, slight acquaintances, or minor but beneficial situations.

Knights

Knights can represent youngish men (sometimes women) or movement in your affairs.

Queens

Queens represent grown women or an aspect of the questioner herself. They rarely represent situations.

Kings

Kings represent mature men or an aspect of the questioner himself, rarely situations.

Major Arcana Cards

A number of these turning up in a reading suggests that fate is taking a hand in a questioner's life. Many of these cards signify new beginnings and the Tarot reader must look at the surrounding Minor Arcana cards to discover exactly what these events and changes of circumstances are referring to.

Ratios

Many Major Arcana cards in a reading suggest that fate is in charge of your life at the time of the reading; mostly Minor Arcana cards in the reading suggest that you are in charge.

HOW TO READ THE CARDS

A NEW DECK

There is a theory that it is unlucky to buy your own Tarot cards, but this is pure superstition. Professionals treat themselves to new and interesting decks all the time. You can keep your cards in any kind of box or bag and wrap them in a piece of silk if you like. I keep mine in a collection of attractive boxes without wrapping them in silk.

If you have a new deck, do ask your spiritual guides to bless the cards before you begin to use them. If you enjoy meditating, hold the cards while doing so. Shuffle them over and over again to mix them thoroughly, to wear off the newness and to put your own 'vibes' on them.

BEFORE READING THE CARDS

Sit down in a quiet place and relax your mind for a moment or two, if you wish you can ask your guides for a blessing. Shuffle the cards and then cut them twice, using the left hand and moving the cut towards the left. Put the cards back together again and proceed by taking them from the top of the deck. You can read the cards for yourself, but you will probably get better results if you read them for someone else and then ask them to read them for you.

Reading the Cards

TAROT SPREADS

There are as many Tarot layouts as there are Tarot readers and you will soon discover those that suit you best. There are generalized spreads that look at your life as a whole, spreads that focus on a particular problem and spreads that offer an indication of timing of events. It is probably best to begin with a generalized spread and then focus down onto a specific problem.

SIGNIFICATORS

You can choose a card to signify a particular person or a particular situation. For example, if you want to look at someone's boyfriend, choose a card that seems to suit his personality, while if you want to look into the chances of finding a good job, choose a card that indicates work or money. Once you have selected a significator, lay it on the table and carry out the reading on top of it.

General Spreads

SPHERES OF LIFE SPREAD

Choose seven positions that represent various areas of your life and lay down a card for each one of these. A typical choice might be:

1 Love
2 Work
3 Money
4 Family
5 Health
6 Travel
7 Home

1   2   3   4   5   6   7

PAST, PRESENT AND FUTURE SPREAD

Draw several cards to represent the past, several more for the present and another batch for the future.

     Past

Present

Future

Focused Spreads

THE 'CONSEQUENCES' SPREAD

If you wish to look at a particular question, the seven-card "consequences" spread is as good as any.

1   The person or the predicament
2   Factors for or against the person or predicament
3   Past influences
4   Future influences
5   Advice on the most useful course of action
6   Surrounding people or circumstances
7   The outcome

3

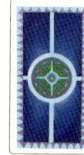

2

4

1

5

6

7

THE CELTIC CROSS

This layout is familiar to every professional Tarot reader, albeit with minor differences due to personal preference. This is not an easy spread for a complete beginner, but you can work up to this when you are more used to the cards.

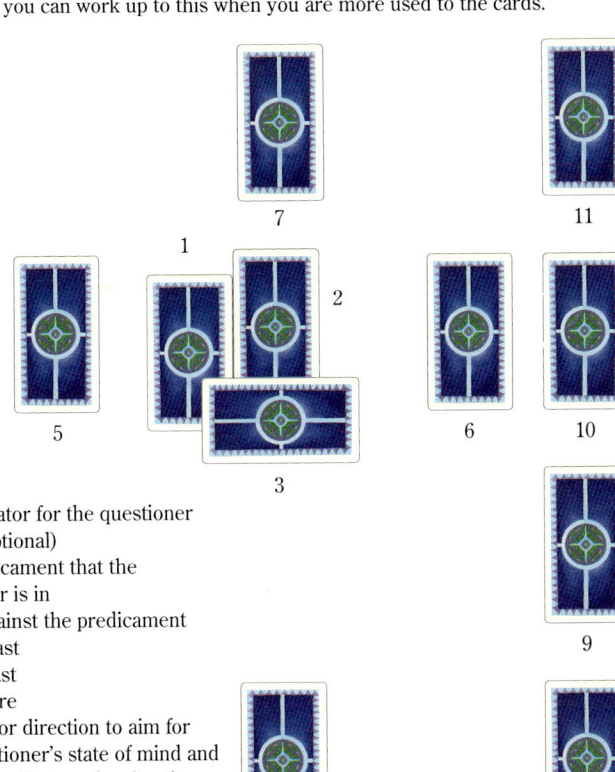

1 A significator for the questioner (this is optional)
2 The predicament that the questioner is in
3 For or against the predicament
4 Distant past
5 Recent past
6 Near future
7 The goal or direction to aim for
8 The questioner's state of mind and his or her effect on the situation
9 The effect of others on the situation, or other environmental factors
10 Hopes, wishes and fears
11 The outcome

Ashley's Reading

After being made redundant from his job, Ashley moved from the country to the city and has just started a business of his own. He would like to know whether his fledgling business will be a success.

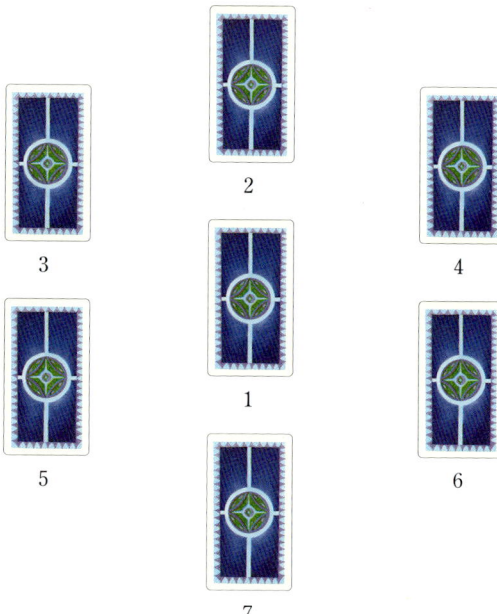

1   King of Pentacles, reversed (Person or predicament)
2   Five of Wands (Factors for or against)
3   The Chariot (Past influence)
4   Seven of Swords (Future influence)
5   Strength (Course of action)
6   Judgement (Environment and other people)
7   Seven of Pentacles (Outcome)

There are three Major Arcana cards and four Minor Arcana cards in this spread, suggesting a balance between Ashley's decisions and the forces of fate.

1   The King of Pentacles shows that Ashley is a competent businessman, but he may be more attuned to finance and accountancy than to manufacturing or salesmanship. The reversal of this card suggests that his budget is a tight one.

2   The Five of Wands suggests that Ashley is optimistic about the challenges that lie ahead.

3   The Chariot denotes important moves, changes, journeys and decisions that have already taken place. Any uncertainty that he may have felt has now gone.

4   The Seven of Swords warns Ashley to guard against being too trusting. He must also accept that even his present situation is very fluid and that he must be prepared to change gear quickly if necessary.

5   The Strength card advises Ashley that endurance will bring results.

6   The Judgement card shows that Ashley can't go back to whatever he was doing before, so he may as well go forward.

7   The Seven of Pentacles assures success, as long as Ashley is prepared to work very hard indeed.

TIME AND THE TAROT

If you need a reading that will give you specific timing of an event, Tarot won't pinpoint this in the way that astrology or numerology will. You can, however, discover which season of the year is likely to be a turning point by designating each of the four suits of the Minor Arcana to a season. In this system, Wand cards represent spring, Cups summer, Pentacles autumn and Swords winter.

To find the point of year for a particular event, shuffle the cards and then take the first card from the top of the deck. If this is a Minor Arcana card, the suit will give you the answer, but if a Major Arcana card shows up, set it aside for a moment. If a second or even a third Major Arcana card shows up, set them all aside and keep going until the first Minor Arcana card turns up. Then go back and look up the meanings of any Major Arcana cards that you have set aside, because any card that brings itself to your attention needs consideration.

A second and very simple way to time events is to lay the cards out in a row with each card representing a month to come. Start with the month you are in, then look up the meaning of each card to see what each month holds, taking special note of those months which are marked by Major Arcana cards, as these show the important months. Certain of the Major Arcana cards emphasize change, so if any month the following cards appear, these months will be memorable:

- **The Fool** represents a fresh start
- **The Wheel of Fortune** represents a change of fortune
- **Death** represents an ending
- **The World** represents completion.

Using both Major and Minor Arcana cards, you can pick out particular situations. For example, if you are keen to know when you are likely to move house, take note of those cards that represent property, if you are interested in travel, note down the months in which travel cards appear. If you want to change your job, then look out for work or money cards, and if love is your goal, then look for cards that denote love.